An architecture for good decision-making

(Originally published by Gopher Publishers in 2000:
ISBN 90-76249-74-1)

© Jeremy Clare 2003

This edition by "Whatever Next….?" Limited

in association with Librario Publishing Limited

ISBN: 1-904440-15-0

Further copies can be obtained from:

Librario Publishing: www.librario.com

By email sales@librario.com

tel: +44 (0) 1343 550245
fax: +44 (0) 1343 550781

or from the author:

jc@whatevernextltd.co.uk

"Whatever Next…." ® is a private limited Company
Number 3715080

To Kate,
my darling wife and companion,
who has helped me in so many ways to tackle
whatever next in life

Acknowledgements

This is hard to write because I know that it is impossible to acknowledge by name all those who have contributed to this book. Family and friends, colleagues and clients, you have encouraged me so much, many of you without knowing it. The writers of the books, poems and songs that I have quoted and acknowledged in the text itself have been enormously helpful just by writing what they have written. To all these people I want to say a big thank you for your contributions and, to those able to read the end result, I hope you enjoy the book!

There is a special additional acknowledgement, however, which does demand one name to be named and that is Mike O'Sullivan. He is mentioned several times in the book but I want to say more. Without him there would be no book because he was instrumental in initiating the whole "Whatever Next….?" concept with me during 1995. He has challenged and encouraged me every step of the way and has helped me to develop in practice many of the principles and processes spelt out inside these covers. He has been my co-facilitator on nearly all of the dozens of workshops held to date. Much more than any of this, however, is the fact that Mike has been such an honest and true friend through it all. I look forward to sharing with him the continuing story following the publication of this book.

Foreword

"It is far more important that one's life should be perceived than that it should be transformed, for no sooner has it been perceived than it transforms itself of its own accord".

   Maurice Maeterlinck (1896)

(This piece of wisdom, now from the century before last, is a key to an understanding of this book. Reading and re-reading it from time to time will bring rewards. It is at the heart of why "Whatever Next....?" was developed, first as a working model for facilitating workshops, and now in book form).

On 21st May 2000 I spent the day on a small group workshop in Latimer, Buckinghamshire, with four others including my co-facilitator and colleague, Mike O'Sullivan, a man of many talents and a very big heart for people and their personal development. The workshop was called **"Whatever Next....?"**. We worked on future plans for all of us there; it was the latest in a monthly series of events using that name and involving a very wide range of participants of all ages.

   Just five years earlier, in May 1995, Mike and I discovered a startling truth about ourselves and have since found it to be true of many, many others. We worked more effectively, more creatively, and more decisively on such a day without a fixed agenda! As we considered the future, and potential decisions to be made, an agenda didn't help. It tended to limit our ideas, our energy, our sense of anticipation of what was possible, our freedom of thought and our enthusiasm. Agendas tend to be based on what is already known - working creatively on what was not yet known turned out to be much more fun!

Good decision-making requires an accurate perception, from a number of angles, of the issue or issues concerned. This is paramount – once that perception is clear then necessary changes, decisions and actions seem to follow much more naturally. Gaining accurate perception is not easy to do alone and unaided – other people, and different methods of thinking about the same issue, both help. Most of the development work for this approach has been in the area of personal decision making, not organisational, but the principles are offered to be examined and tested in any setting.

And now, nearly three years after I wrote this foreword for the first time, it's time for a second edition. **"Whatever Next….?"** is going strong. There are several events each month and a number of facilitators involved. The ideas behind the original workshop have been developed in all sorts of ways and the future is rapidly filling with exciting possibilities.

If you are interested in finding out more then do visit the website and/or email me at jc@whatevernextltd.co.uk

Jeremy Clare
April 2003

A note about quotations, references and trees!

As you work through this book you will notice a good number of references to literature, poetry and verse, including some from the Bible. Hopefully you will find many of the quotations relevant to your own situation. You may be puzzled as to why Biblical material has been used. It is simply that my own journey has led me that way. I do want, however, to make it plain that you certainly do not need to be a Christian, nor indeed a follower of any religion, to use and benefit from this book. You simply need to be someone who wants to be more actively and consciously engaged in your own life, seeking answers to your own questions, and looking for a better way of finding them.

The chestnut tree at my garden gate provided inspiration for the seasonal themes which run through the book

Contents

Introduction

A close colleague of mine encouraged me to tell you that you really ought to read this book – but what sort of a book is it?

It is an account of some of the journeys we all need to make in coming to good decisions......at the right time...... in both our life and in our work..... and in an increasingly fast-moving, uncertain and disrupted world.

In some of those situations we will find that we don't actually have to make any decision at all – things just happen.

Many find today's fast-moving environment confusing, difficult, even hostile, and we need to understand more about why this is so. At least part of the answer may be found to be cultural. Traditional Western, and especially British, values of self-confidence, self-sufficiency, independence, knowing the "right" thing to do and then doing it – all these come under pressure in the face of today's potent mixture of paradox and complexity. Ethical, technological and "pace of change" issues abound and press in on us every day. Knowledge is not in short supply, but perhaps wisdom is. The whole information-rich, but highly muddled, scenario can easily render us *not* knowing what to do! This can produce anxiety, stress and a certain impotence in decision-making – even a tendency to "freeze" altogether.

The original impetus for the book came from hundreds of career development encounters with individuals and groups since the early 1990s, encounters consisting of conversations, consultancy, counselling, coaching and just plain chat! It has become evident to me that many very able, intelligent and industrious people find themselves having great difficulty deciding "Whatever Next....?" in their own lives.

One part of the problem seems to be the complexity of what is potentially out there for them. For example, when I wrote the first edition in 1999, Internet start-ups, sometimes known as dot.coms, seemed to be the new (and to many unknown) area of discovery and possibility. To some this was exciting, challenging and energising, to others it helped not a whit to know that that there was yet another subject of worldwide significance that they didn't know enough about! Another part of the problem is the nature of continuous change which, of course, has always been present to some extent but which is now taking place at a giddying, sometimes frightening pace. Working scenarios have altered so much that, for many people emerging from their current workplaces, it is difficult to recognise the surrounding landscape, even in their "own" industry or sector.

Faced with the confusion of not knowing how to proceed, and especially in making big decisions over our future life and/or work, there is a tendency to adopt one of any number of dysfunctional approaches. Some common examples are listed below:

Stay put - "better the devil you (think!) you know..."

Jump - often without proper consideration – a major risk of "out of the frying pan into the fire".

Worry - with an overtone of "it will probably get worse anyway"....this is often allied with "freezing".

Float - "better not to know what's going on, it'll all sort itself out in the end"...a relaxed position, but vulnerable

Hide - "if they don't notice me perhaps I will escape the turmoil unscathed, and thus won't have to make a decision!"

Although there is a modicum of wisdom in each of these attitudes, none could really be considered a coherent approach to personal decision-making for the year 2003 and beyond. It is my hope that this book, with the outline philosophy and methods that it suggests, will be a help to those who recognise some of those symptoms that are alluded to above.

If the book is to work well for you, you need to understand how to use it best. Remember that this is a working, living book for you to <u>use</u>, hence the numerous blank pages for your notes. Tackling the questions will reap dividends.

Three principles are important and need to be understood:

1. **This is a book that is best shared with others.** It would be more than useful for you to purchase a second copy which I encourage you to give (or sell!) to another person with whom you can talk things through. You will be an enormous help to one another as you each work your way through the book and discuss some of your responses to the ideas contained in it.

2. **Start the book wherever you like**. In the next section you will find a description of how the book is divided up into four "seasons" of three chapters each. There are 12 Chapters and, with the possible exception of the currently empty Chapter 11, anywhere can be a good

place to start. You could even start by using those blank pages of Chapter 11 to illustrate or to write about an issue which faces you at the outset, and then move off from there – "Whatever Next....?" in action!

3. **I believe that we are we are made up of body, mind, soul and spirit** and that we need to recognise all those parts of us as a whole. Don't be too surprised, therefore, by the many and varied themes drawn from philosophers, psychologists, poets, singers, soldiers and writers of spiritual and religious literature. Living out my own life as a Christian, my personal frame of reference will become evident as you read your way through. Your own frame of reference, however, is the one you are going to work with and will be different. I hope that the variety of quotes will appeal, for each of us is unique. None of us has a monopoly of wisdom! Add your own favoured writings to those already within these pages.

I would commend the writer CS Lewis' suggestion that if we don't believe, then at least we agree to suspend *dis* belief while we read. We really can get to grips with the contents of this book and make excellent use of it, regardless of whether we think of ourselves as "believers".

Now it's time to get going! Read again the quote in the foreword from Maurice Maeterlinck and think about it some more – it provides a key which you will learn to turn to good effect as you unlock the "Whatever Next....?" approach.

Bon voyage!

Alternative places to get started

You can just read away from Chapter 1 as with any other book, but if you look in the Contents Page you will see that the chapters are divided into four "seasons" each with a rather different emphasis. The short introductions below may encourage you to start where you feel it's most appropriate for you personally, and then read on round the seasons in their natural order, finishing wherever you want to stop!

Autumn entry (Chapter 1)

Many of these people will probably be excited, puzzled, anxious or perturbed either by their own world, the wider world or both. Difficult or painful events may have dominated their lives recently – things happening which have brought a feeling of uncertainty and insecurity to the fore. Whereas there have been times in the relatively recent past when everything was fine, or seemed fine, the feeling now is that life is on the turn, like Autumn. The leaves are getting a brownish tinge and strong winds are blowing – this turbulence prompts the question:

"What's going on here?"

A sense of needing to do some stocktaking is apparent, a desire to address the puzzling issues and to find out more about the nature of the uncertainty, particularly what it means to you personally. There is a desire also to discover the *root* of any anxiety and to relate whatever is uncovered to their thinking about the future.

Winter entry (Chapter 4)

Things may seem pretty bleak for these readers. There could be a rather spartan quality to life at the moment which may suggest that there were better times in the past, but which on reflection also speaks of better times ahead.

Could it be that the best is yet to come? It is time to dig deep and turn over the soil. Perhaps it is time to inspect roots and foundations for security? Time to ponder anew before considering the next step? This requires both thought and a sense of vision – fortunately the visibility is often good in winter when there are no leaves on the trees!

An appreciation will be needed both of where you have been in seasons past and the destination you seek to reach in the next phase of your life. The thought of all that thinking may be daunting! The question that causes many to hesitate is:

"Where shall I start?"

You may be on a journey but currently feel that you are stranded on a plateau on some remote mountain. You may feel you have set out on a voyage but are currently stuck on a sandbank awaiting the rescuing effect of tide or wind to move you on. With or without metaphors to help you, what should you do next? Make whatever preparations you can to move on and discover by talking to others that this is not such a lonely place after all.

*Others are around who can help, so don't try to puzzle **all** of it out on your own!*

Spring entry (Chapter 7)
This person is already in optimistic and opportunistic mood, excited by the future but maybe hesitant about exactly what to do about it! Hesitant also, maybe, about whether he or she is about to do the "right" thing, whether

he *should* do it, whether he can, whether he ought to or whether he really wants to. The right seeds are all in place but the confidence level about taking the decisions and getting on with things is on the low side. The result may thus be inaction and mental foot-dragging. One of the key questions may well be:

"How do I get there?"

Remember that it is only that vital first step that needs to be taken in order to start the journey. This person needs moral support, feedback, encouragement and a watering of the seeds. She needs people to ask the right questions and get her properly in touch with what she wants to achieve. Energy and potential are much in evidence but the sense of purpose and direction are partly lacking. Remember that plants need to grow downward (roots) as well as upwards!

Summer entry (Chapter 10)

Here we may find people who might already be engaged in meaningful activity and who are finding satisfaction in that activity, whatever it is. If they work, then that work may be paid or unpaid, full-time or part-time, indoors or outdoors, home or office based. However, this person needs to enjoy the flowering of their own endeavours and to get full benefit from that – both from a personal perspective and from what it can do for others. Their issue is probably not so much to do with the "rightness" of a current situation or direction as with discovering its full potential and, importantly, where it might lead to. A number of keynote questions may arise:

"What shall I do now?" or possibly *"Where am I right now?"* or perhaps *"What else do I want to do?"*

These may be important questions in a "summer-flowering" or "full leaf" situation. There is an awareness that autumn will probably come next! Life is seasonal and rhythmical and there is a time for every purpose under heaven – this was much sung about by Peter, Paul and Mary in the Sixties and, very much earlier, in the book of Ecclesiastes! Currently there may be a need to enjoy what's going on at present, but also to review the fruits of current and past effort – not just to rest on laurels but also to look ahead for future direction.

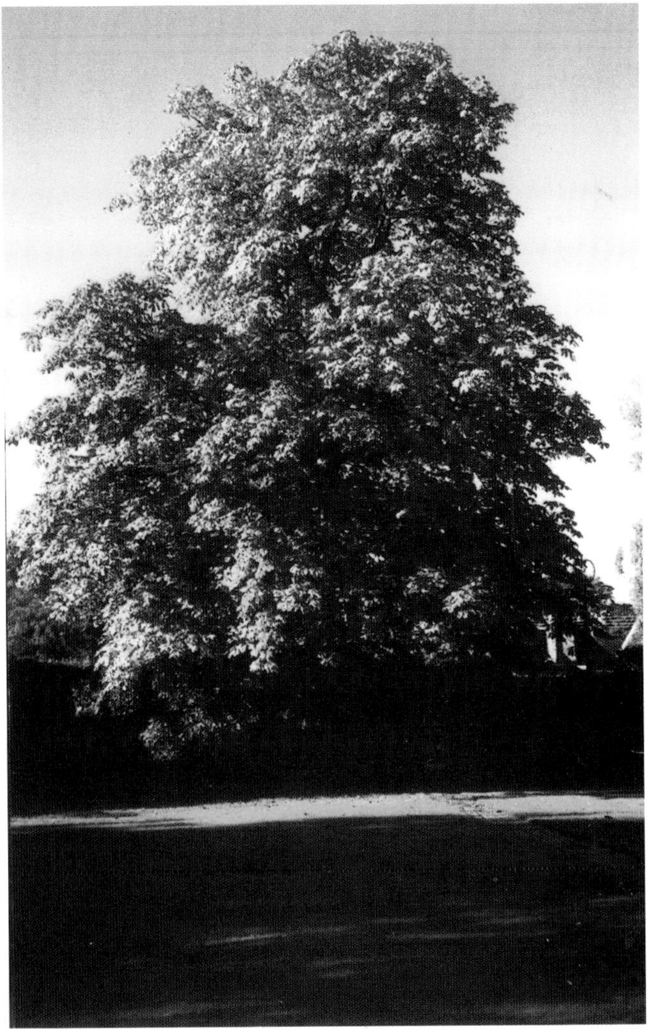

Chapter 1

Knowing and not knowing

(Season: "Autumn" Key question: "What is going on here?")

"Whatever Next....?" If we knew the answer to that question we would not bother to ask it. Indeed, the question itself would never have occurred to us in the first place. We do not know the future with certainty, even the immediate future, and so the question is always a valid one. Much of the time we like to think that we are pretty confident we know what is coming in the days and years ahead. We will tend to make our plans accordingly, based on what we *believe* to be so. But supposing we are wrong?

Our thinking patterns often lead us to suppose that if we *knew*, really knew, then all would be well. But what if we actually knew the future to be abysmal for us, and far too difficult to plan for? That is an unpalatable thought that would lead to immense worry and stress. Our tendency, therefore, is often to try to construct a future in our minds based on templates as close as possible to those with which we are already familiar, and then to do all we can to preserve those templates. Then, we tell ourselves, the future will be reasonably understandable, as comfortable as the past, or not much less so. An approach that consists primarily of trying to conserve around us a familiar *status quo*, is not a good general tactic for the likely turmoil of the 21st century. Some would maintain that it has never been a good philosophy in any era and is bound to fail!

Things are changing too fast, both technologically and ethically. Too little is commonly accepted as the norm. Too few agree as to what is truly desirable to maintain without change. As a result, the outcome of such a tactic is likely to be a state of almost permanent alarm at the unsettled nature of what is up ahead. In a recent straw poll the majority view of several hundred people present was that the new century would probably get progressively worse compared with the previous one. A hundred years ago, in a far more optimistic age, a similar poll would almost certainly have said the reverse, i.e. things are very likely to get progressively better.

If we are going to live sanely and cheerfully in a progressively unstable world, we need to come to terms with the continual paradox and mess and to become more comfortable with the idea of *not* knowing! Captain Cook discovered Botany Bay when he didn't even know it was there – that should be an encouragement for all of us. He did not have to know all about the Bay in advance in order to map out the rest of his trip, or his life. Once he had discovered it, however, he could then consider how it might change the future for him and his crew and take appropriate action.

In my work I frequently come across people who are trying to do one of two things. Either they are trying to reproduce the past for their comfort and security, or alternatively they are seeking something different but without a notion of what they are looking for, or how to set about the task. A client who had been made redundant told me recently, "for 20 years I've known I want to do something else and I still have no idea what it is!"

What is our inclination in such situations? Often it is to seek many different strands of external opinion and advice

– to listen to almost anyone or anything that might point us in the "right" direction. What on earth do we mean by "right" in this context? Have we even tried listening quietly for the authoritative voice of our "inner self", all too often drowned-out by the potent combination of previous experience and the insistent expectations of others. Do we, for example, believe in guidance from God and if so, have we sought it through meditation or listening prayer?

It has been wisely said:
Listen to the knowing in your heart before speaking from the learning in your head

It has also been wisely (but at this stage maybe provocatively) said:
Everyone knows the answers to their own questions about themselves

Milton Erikson, the psychologist and therapist, maintained that it was not he but every individual client who was the real expert on his or her own case. As far as choosing a way ahead for our own work/life is concerned, I believe this generally to be true – the answers are in all of us and they need careful teasing out. I hope this book will help you to ask appropriate questions of yourself, and then to answer them over time.

The main purpose of "Whatever Next....?" is to spark an interest in a very different approach to what we do not know. At the core of this approach is the realisation that alongside the oft-asked question **"What *should* I do?"** there is also a range of other questions that are just as valid. They need to be addressed alongside the "shoulds and oughts" of life. They include the following and it would be useful to reflect on each question in turn and make a few notes in immediate response:

in my future:

"What must I do?"

"What do I need to do?"

"What can I do?"

"What could I do?"

"What would I like to do?"

"What do I want to do?"

"What would I *really* love to do?"

*(Note that the questions **"What should I do?" or "What ought I to do?** probably fit in between "need" and "can" in this series. Is there anything in that category for you? Are you sure it really is in that category? Where have the "shoulds" come from?)*

Uncertainty and, specifically, the fear of uncertainty that we discuss at some length in the next chapter, is the bogey man for many, and the bogey person for the politically correct! The fear of uncertainty paralyses many people's lives today. In the face of *not* knowing, our default thinking needs to become "I'll find out!" rather than "I can't move". We do not need either to settle for, or to try to manufacture, the *status quo*. We cannot receive new things, new ideas, new ways of looking at situations or completely new thoughts if we are too chock full of the old ones and unwilling to relinquish any of them.

This book is about discovering truths, not inventing new ones. There are no new truths in existence, merely new aspects of those that have been there since time began. How do we set about revealing new aspects of what we need to know in our lives? We go looking, asking, seeking, knocking; we turn back covers, we unfold maps, we turn over dead leaves and see what is underneath; we right upturned boats and re-launch them so that we can get a view of the mainland from a different direction. Perhaps we have been hanging around on dry land too long and need to go for an exhilarating sail!

In order to do all this we need a generous measure of humility; we need to pay attention to the effect of our own pride that Ted Hughes expresses so graphically in the poem "Hawk roosting". Are not many of us a bit like this hawk, sitting and surveying the world beneath him?

Nothing has changed since I began,
My eye has permitted no change,
I'm going to keep things like this.

We need to become more content with the changing of the seasons in our lives, just as we accept that Nature's four seasons will continue to roll around, come what may. This first chapter is an "autumn" chapter. Autumn is a fine season and John Keats wrote a famous ode on the subject to tell us so! In our own autumn, let's not ask, "Where are the songs of spring?" but rather follow his advice and enjoy right now the "barred clouds that bloom in the soft dying day and touch the stubbled plain with rosy hue". A key to successful decision-making is the serene acceptance of what we cannot change. We need to accept "that which we are, we are", and to start from here – it's generally the best place to start!

CS Lewis, in his reflections on the Psalms, noted that he often found it more beneficial to seek the help of the pupil rather than that of the master. He noted that the fellow pupil is often able to help us more because he knows less.

I encourage you to join with all life's fellow pupils in experimenting with this approach, striking out tired old agendas and well-worn presuppositions about what's possible in the future and instead tackling our "Whatever Next....?" questions in an honest, straightforward and expectant spirit of discovery.

Questions to ponder:

Which of those things that currently concern me in my life/situation could I change?

Which, of those things that I could change, do I really *want* to change?

What can I *not* change?

Notes:

Chapter 2

Fear

(Season: "Autumn" Key question: "What is going on here?")

I want to return for a moment to what we might term the prevailing *mood* in our society and to pose again the question mentioned in Chapter 1, "Are things getting progressively worse, staying much the same or getting progressively better?" I sense in many people a sort of confused admiration for much that is happening in science, medicine and technology, but at the same time an anxious questioning about where it is all leading. There is a deep and understandable concern about the lack of ethical frameworks for much of what is being developed. Do we fear that despite the burgeoning power of western economies, the brilliance of research scientists and surgeons, the immense creativity and intelligence of many of our brightest stars, the dazzling possibilities of the Internet and of the world wide web, things may actually get *worse*, not better? We hope things will get better, but that hope is not a sure and certain expectancy – it is rather the guarded, doubtful and somewhat hesitant optimism of the English phrase "I hope so".

A fear element often accompanies the uncertainty of it all, and anxiety often derives from a feeling of personal powerlessness to affect events. Life could not be lived without a healthy measure of stress in our lives, deriving from those basic survival instincts of the primitive "fight or flight" decisions. Those instincts produce much of the adrenalin and energy necessary for tackling difficult situations. But a permanently stressful fear of the unknown is not so healthy – it will tend to condemn us to a consistently fearful attitude in the face of such a fast moving world.

Let's face the truth – we do not know, and cannot know, whether the events which will affect us in the future will be more or less pleasant, very much better or considerably worse. All we can do is to equip ourselves better for *whatever* next, an attitude whereby we can cope effectively with what comes along. I know for myself, and maybe you do too, that the power of Good calls us upwards – "heavenwards" is the expression favoured by St Paul. Evil on the other hand calls us downwards. If we as a people are travelling downwards, that is to say getting progressively worse in a moral and spiritual sense, then surely we should quite logically feel fearful! That downward way is ultimately destructive and leads us to a very negative place or destination....some might even refer to it as hell, however you choose to interpret that word!

Upward-looking, positive and optimistic attitudes, not Polyanna-ish attitudes but those firmly rooted in historical perspective and common sense, are thus to be encouraged. The second half of life (and I have to assume that I am already there in my early fifties) needs only to be a gentle downwards glide in terms of our physical abilities. That's plain common sense – a decline is bound to happen gradually as our body ages and wears out naturally. Hopefully we can come to accept that with a measure of good grace! Mentally and spiritually, however, this downwards glide is not at all inevitable and most of us will have seen fine examples of continuous, positive progress in these realms, right into the final weeks of other people's lives.

It is worth asking an appropriate question at this juncture:

What exactly do we fear?

Many fear failure......but what if we fail in a genuine endeavour? Well now, think about that..... what if we do? At least we made the endeavour and will have lived through it and gained much from the experience. Perhaps our fears would be lessened if we adopted as our goal not to live long but to live *now!* Karl Menninger wrote that:

Fears can be educated into us and they can, if we wish, be educated out.

A question to ponder for a minute: have you got your own personal values and agendas by which you are living your life? The answer is probably yes, but are you aware of exactly what your values are, and where they came from? Do you feel that your agendas are mostly external and imposed upon you, or are you aware of having set them for yourself? Are they up to date and are they what is appropriate for you now, at this stage in your life?

You may well be striving towards a position or status in life, a major success, a large salary, a lovely house, a comfortable retirement or all of the above! Are these the things that you, you inside, the real you in your heart of hearts, actually want most out of life? Are you running in the rat race because you filled in the entry form yourself, or because someone else filled it in for you? And now you are in the race, are you personally enjoying it and gaining fulfilment from finishing, or the anticipation of finishing, in the top flight? I've no idea whether it is possible actually to win the rat race, but as Lily Tomlin once said so pithily, *even if you do win, you're still a rat!*

None of these observations and questions is intended to run counter to the idea of healthy ambition. I work with numerous successful people who want more success, to move onwards and upwards in their career in the conventional sense, as outlined above. If those people have thought it through, are clear about what they are doing and why, and about the net effect on their lives as a whole, then that's great. May they "go for it" with real energy and purpose. The fact of the matter is, however, that many people have *not* thought it through for themselves. They are often living out the expectations of others (parents, spouses, partners or peer groups, perhaps) or, sadly, just copying everyone else!

We often fall into the trap of thinking that the alternative to conventional "success" can only be deemed failure, mostly doom and gloom and definitely second best. There are common measures of a particular type that have consistently promoted such attitudes, typified by what the previous government kept calling the "feel good factor". This always seemed to relate to money and the economy in some way. No one would deny that it is usually easier to live out our lives, and control much of what we want to control in this materialistic world, via a healthy bank balance. However, the anxiety that the only alternative, the inevitable opposite, must be named failure is a complete misuse of our fearful imagination.

The simplistic argument says that if we are not conventional successes we must be conventional failures! Why instead can we not be unconventional successes?

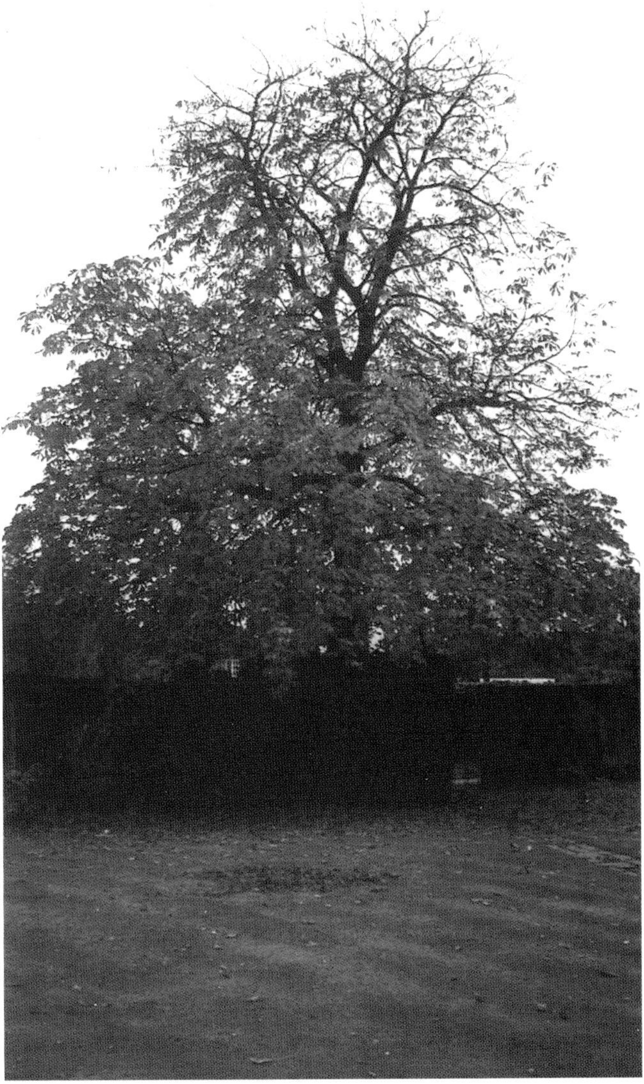

Maybe those unconventional successes will have succeeded in the agendas that they have set *themselves*, perhaps with the help of a radically different value system. In order to overcome anxiety and fear about the uncertainties ahead, we need to gain control over this area of our judgement and "Whatever Next....?" wants to make a contribution to that process. Think carefully now:

... is what you choose to do next likely to be ruled by a should, a could, a must, an ought to, a need to – or will it be what you really want to do?

The reality is that there will probably be some of each, but have you paid proper attention to what you *really* want to do, while trusting that you will still attend to your genuine and worthwhile responsibilities in life. What is the balance like? We cannot always do what we want to do, that's true, but on the other hand are we only allowed to do what we *ought* to do? Why? Who says? Whose "ought" is this? Have we really thought it through?

Author's note: *In case you have not yet noticed, there are a lot of questions in the early part of this book! Oscar Wilde once wrote that it is always worth asking a question, though it is not always worthwhile answering one! There is a great deal of truth in that; sometimes the question is infinitely more important. Keep framing the appropriate question for yourself.*

Stick with it and start working in the spaces for your notes on coming up with some or part of your answers, but only as the picture becomes clearer to you. My experience with many people tells me that it will not necessarily happen today...or even tomorrow! Take heart however from the fact that we do have most of the answers, even if they are often buried well under the surface. Start digging 'em up.

And now let's change tack completely and consider a statistic, in fact it's really the ultimate statistic for the mathematically challenged:

One out of every one of us will die!

Death is the end of our physical story. I was prompted to write those words down "live", just as the first news of a dreadful train crash in West London was coming over the radio in October 1999. Many had been killed instantly as fire had completely engulfed a whole carriage. Since then the huge scale of the events of September 11th 2001, the Bali bombings and the war in Iraq have somewhat overtaken the collective memory. Such violent and sudden death could be a fearful way to end our story, unless we know a bigger and better story of which our story is just a part. In the light of the truth that we will all die one day, and that none of us has any idea when, what else do you want to do with your life?

I say "want" quite deliberately, but not in a hedonistic, self-centred sense. What is your vision of how you would like your life to be in a few years time? Do you fear that you cannot achieve that? Have you already "butted" it out of your mind (e.g. "I'd really like to work abroad but...")? I genuinely dislike that word "but" in this sort of context, because it is constantly undermining our real hopes and aspirations. It is constantly giving us reasons why we can't, and in truth few of them are really good reasons!

We need to learn more about deciding, and also what to decide, and also how to decide. We also need to understand the value of waiting and not deciding yet. . I believe that this book, and any "Whatever Next....?" workshops, walks, weekends or other events which may supplement it for you, will help you in deciding. They will also help you in selecting those elements of your future which it is *within* your power to choose, and to accept those that are not... and to understand the difference. Feeling powerless, trapped and experiencing events as being totally out of control eventually leads to extreme anxiety and even an abject fear of life itself. There are skills involved in taking more control and responsibility – skills that can be learned. There is a robust attitude to uncertainty that works well for most people and situations, neatly summed up by Susan Jeffers' book title *Feel the fear and do it anyway.*

As a reader of the Bible, I have noticed that two of the most frequently used greetings from God to man in the Biblical account are "Fear not" and "Don't be afraid". This was said to Abraham, Moses, Joshua, the Shepherds, Joseph and Mary, to name but a few. I notice that all of them were on the threshold of the unknown and all were filled with uncertainty about what was required of them. I think we can learn something important about ourselves from the way that God used those greetings.

That leads to two important questions to ponder:

"What exactly am I afraid of in my situation?"

"What would I do if I were not afraid?"

Notes:

Chapter 3

Signs of the times

(Season: "Autumn"   Key question: "What is going on here?")

Having proposed in the last chapter that many people find the world of 2000 and beyond an anxiety producing place, let us look at the sorts of things that are worrying us. David Cormack, a writer and keen thinker about the future, suggests "We are faced with a crisis of ten thousand changes." Our world has been rocked by a series of revolutions – political, sexual, technological and environmental. Changes of all kinds are transforming our familiar reference points. Even changes for the better are happening too fast. Instead of being victims of change, Cormack insists we can learn to be agents of change, or at least participative actors *in* change. We need to make friends with "the big question marks that dominate the skyline". If we do not participate, Cormack warns that we will be swamped and crushed by change. That's fearful!

Talking of crushing puts me in mind of earthquakes, hurricanes and collapsing buildings, foundations shaking and walls giving way. There have been many natural disasters in recent years. There have also been many wars and rumours of wars. At the time of writing Kosovo, East Timor, Sudan and Chechnya have been much in the news. As I make a few final revisions before publication the action (or the media attention) has switched to Sierra Leone, Eritrea, Zimbabwe and Sri Lanka. These have been the high profile stories attracting the western media, and of course there are numerous less publicised conflicts all around the globe. There have also been many major accidents in recent years, many of tragic proportions. Does all this mean anything or are we just going through a "bad patch"? Is there a bigger story?

There is a biblical account of future events that sound very similar to many of those outlined above. Are we actually experiencing part of what we read about in the Gospels, Jesus speaking as recorded in Matthew Chapter 24 or Luke Chapter 22 – Christ's account of what have come to be known as the end times? The news of many current disasters certainly resonates if one is familiar with the text. As a Christian I believe these readings to be highly relevant to understanding a very confusing world, but what difference does that understanding make?

Well, of course it could lead to sitting and waiting, doing nothing, fatalistically bracing ourselves for the final crunch. That is surely a poor way to live, robbing ourselves of all the good times we could enjoy now, in deference to a permanent knawing anxiety about the future. If, however, prophetic words give us a sense of proportion, a sense of urgency that whatever we want to do with our lives, we'd better get on with it, then they will have served us well. Jesus always gave the impression that he knew what he was talking about. It was said of him that he spoke as a man of authority. Far from a view that God is allowing things to fall apart, Paul wrote "in Him all things hold together". Jesus' predictions in the Gospels can give *us* a sense of knowing a little about what is happening, and also provide an introduction to a much bigger and more important story which cannot be related here, but to which I shall refer from time to time.

The last few paragraphs may have raised questions in your minds. They may have just rendered you incredulous that anyone could consider biblical prophecy relevant to the modern world! Well, try returning to those big questions, questions about how we come to terms with the tangled issues of ethical vacuums, rampant technological advance, wars, disasters and suffering. How can we make sense of any of all this? Materialism and the increased prosperity that we currently experience in the West will not even attempt to address those questions. The answers cannot be bought.

Roger Scruton, writer and philosopher, has wisely observed that we are gaining "an increasing grasp of the means to attain our goals and a decreasing grasp of the reason for pursuing those goals in the first place". This contains echoes of TS Eliot who wrote that "we had the experience but never found the meaning".

So then, what *is* the significance of "the times" in considering the "Whatever Next....?" question for ourselves. It is by being aware of today, right now....

- We have no other present day in which to plan, to change or to live out our priorities for our time on earth.

- Our lives are not a dress rehearsal; we only get one go!

- We can only start from where we are.

In one sense therefore, the times are irrelevant. However, in the larger story we have a limited window (and we do not know how limited) in which to slot our own contribution to life and to the lives of those around us. If, as some would maintain, the world itself has a sell-by date, how can we be sure to *live* our lives and not just wait for the end.

Montaigne wrote that a man may live long but yet live very little. We need to get on with living our lives to the full and that will involve both good decision-making and much use of our willpower! Do we really want to assign our personal future to an impersonal mélange of fate and chance, imperfectly commentated upon by a horoscope? Do we not really believe, deep down, that there *is* "a time for every purpose under heaven"? If we want to take our part in those purposes, we first need to take time to find out what this part of ours is all about.

Alvin Toffler's book "Future Shock", much read and admired in the late Seventies, accurately predicted many of the situations we are now facing. We can continue making enlightened predictions about the external factors that may well come to bear on us individually and as a society. Some element of foresight and intelligent anticipation helps us, even if only in "fight or flight" mode! However, the internal world of our perceptions – how we face up to not knowing what will happen, to the fear of uncertainty, to the perceived worsening of many trends and situations – these are not helped by horoscopes or soothsayers. Both the internal and the external world need a more accurate understanding of the human nature that we all inhabit in common.

I want to set out a simple working hypothesis, and not an original one. We are imperfect creatures, but always capable of greater things. We are not solo acts, we need others to help bring out our full potential and we deeply crave a personal integrity and wholeness which consumer purchases and expensive lifestyles can never offer us. However glitzy, smooth and beguiling the marketing of such things may be, money cannot buy us very much real fulfilment.

In order to become more comfortable with uncertainty, we need to find some form of faith (not necessarily religious), sometimes defined as the evidence of things *not* seen. Such a faith will sustain us in the deserts, bogs, rocky landscapes, storms and fogs of life. We need to learn to "see" where we are going, even when visibility is down to hand in front of face. What forms can such a faith take and how can faith help us? Looking ahead into Chapter 4, where there may be a wintry chill, we realise that it is often the things that we *cannot* see that become the most meaningful, and especially so in crisis. If we are told that our nearest and dearest is terminally ill, neither the bank balance nor the partial knowledge of what is to come will help our spirit. We need faith in a bigger story and a way of ascribing meaning to what is happening. We can only regain our true sense of direction from a very different quality of knowing.

Questions to ponder:

What bothers me particularly about the times we live in, and how do these things actually affect me?

What forms of faith do I exhibit right now and where do I tend to place my trust?

What steps might I take right now to more fully engage with my life/situation?

What resources might I draw upon (e.g: books, courses, particular people)?

Notes:

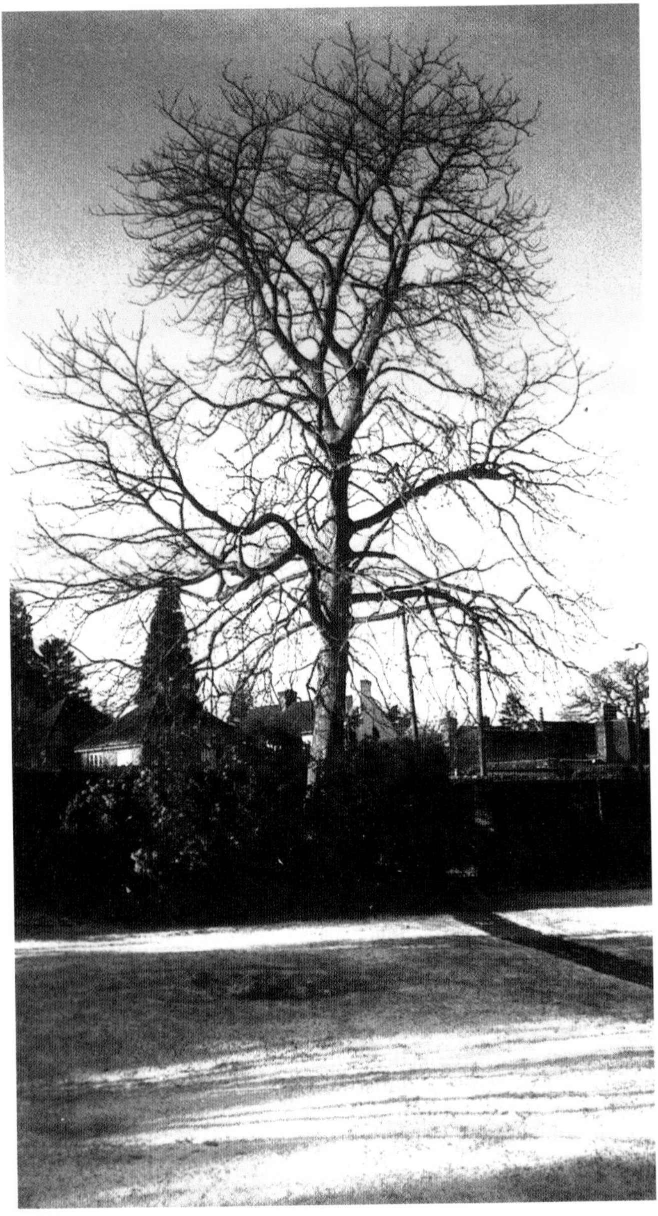

Chapter 4

Faith

(Season: "Winter" Key question: "Where shall I start?")

People often talk of faith as if it is something they either have or haven't got. In fact every one of us has faith in all sorts of things, otherwise we would never go anywhere or do anything at all. Unless we exercised faith both in the lifting power of the airflow over a wing and the training of airline pilots, we would certainly never fly anywhere! What is faith? Well, one useful description comes from the Bible where it is described as being certain of what we cannot actually see. We are convinced of a probability in our minds and then take action on the basis of that conviction (and that alone, otherwise it's not faith).

I have faith that this book is going to get written, though at the stage that I'm writing this early draft in October 1999, this is the first and only paragraph in existence........ this is exactly the point where I have started writing the book (on a pale blue record card while sitting overlooking Loch Achray in Scotland!). To some extent I can picture the book in my mind's eye but actually there is nothing else to see at all yet, except one paragraph of what I believe will become Chapter 4!

In some cases we trust in facts or theories, in other situations we trust our instinct and in still others we trust in the good character of another person. None of these things is visible as such. The link which makes our resultant action decisive is faith. Ask yourself, "In what do I trust, or in whom do I trust?", and then ask what difference the answer makes? We are predicting an outcome based on our faith, and it is an "act of faith" which often helps us in resolving "Whatever Next....?" questions and situations.

It is worth noting that the words faith and hope are not so very far apart in their New Testament (i.e.Greek) meanings. "Elpis" is the Greek for hope, and it meant to have a confident expectation that something *would* actually come to pass, not just an uncertain and vague optimism that it might. That is an important distinction – we do not really use the word hope in that way in modern day English when we say "I hope so".

In faith you act as if something is true. It is the very act of making the choice, of deciding. The choice may, in fact, not be based on a probability at all, just a possibility, in which case the faith component is even greater.

As we decide on an issue concerning the future for ourselves, do we tend to base our decision on our own evaluation, and our own values, or on a sort of gallup poll consensus as to what *should* happen next?

In "Whatever Next....?" workshops, the belief and the consequent act of faith which I have come to put into action personally is this: *that people most often know the answers to their own questions,* and that with the help of others in supportive mode, the answers will eventually be revealed...........at least to those who really want to know the answer.

Faith is not a feeling – you either believe "it" or you don't. If you don't act on your belief, you don't have faith. If you believe some of the time and at other times disbelieve then this is doubt, that is to say, being in two minds. Trying to hold onto two conflicting beliefs at the same time is hard work, and it is common to us all at times. Haven't we all had the experience of being unable to make up our minds as to whether we can, or cannot, do something difficult – and agonised over the decision? It requires an *act of faith* to break the deadlock, not just a change of mind!

"Whatever Next....?" principles (see Chapter 8) will encourage you to face the future with a working faith and to explore the likely results of your choices in a safe place. They will enable you to exercise the faith that you need in a supportive setting, realizing, as John Donne did, that you are not an "island". That safe atmosphere, that supportive setting, might just consist of you and one other person who is as keen as you to explore the possibilities of the future and who agrees to work using the guidelines set out in this book. I'm hoping you have acquired two copies of this book – give one to someone to work with you, or even better, find another pair and work in a foursome.

Doubt is a respectable position, experienced by most of us, but it will not lead us to positive action. Unbelief in our ability concerning a key decision on the future will cement us in the status quo, "I am not absolutely sure that I can do what I want to do, therefore I will not take action". What is the significance of faith in taking or making decisions about the future? Simply this: in the short term it provides a measure of solidity to the next-step decision. An English-style, uncertain "hope" does not provide that platform. Paul wrote to the Corinthians that "it is by faith that you stand firm". By this he implies that it is an exercise of our will, not our intellect. It has a spiritual dimension though it is not a *specifically* religious concept. The Christian faith, for example, contains within it a whole raft of propositions (e.g.

Jesus died and rose again), which if *acted upon* as true, will deeply affect our decision making, indeed our whole lives. A literal life or death situation facing us takes on a completely different complexion if we have genuine faith in our longer term future!

As a last step in this chapter, we need to relate the concept of faith to that of fear, the subject of Chapter Two. Fear is an anticipation that dreaded events (large or small) will, or may, come to pass, perhaps as a result of our own decision. Our fear is that all will not be well. Worry is closely allied to such fear, and is always destructive in nature. Facing the future with faith can mean agreeing with the supposition that there may well be worse times ahead in the shorter term, but not agreeing that prolonged gloom or doom is the inevitable outcome. It is possible to fear, with good reason, and yet not to worry. Susan Jeffers expounds this philosophy in her book, *Feel the Fear and Do It Anyway.* The folk song "We shall overcome", commonly associated with the civil rights movement in the USA in the sixties, was a song of faith, not based on actually experiencing a good outcome but trusting that it would come to pass, that good would eventually triumph over evil. Significantly, that trust resulted in taking *action* as if it were so, and thus demonstrating the proposition to be true in the longer term.

Questions to ponder:

What negative outcomes or possibilities am I currently fearing?

Is there any evidence that the outcomes will definitely be negative?

What other outcomes might equally well occur?

Notes:

Chapter 5

Journeys

(Season: "Winter" Key question: "Where shall I start?")

Let me share some articles of faith which I have taken into use in my own life.......that travelling is at least as important as arriving; that life is as much about journeys as it is about destinations; that how we got here is often just as important as where we have got to. If you are currently in a bleak place in your life, and you're fed up with that place, the first key question is not always, "where do I want to go?" but sometimes more pragmatically, "how do I get moving?". To make the decisions that will take us out of a difficult patch, we need the willingness and the energy to move on mentally. We also need to adopt a real attitude of faith that we *will* in fact get to a different place over time. The willingness, the mental energy and the act of faith combine to provide the fuel required for the journey.

In this opening paragraph of the chapter, I have used some picture language to describe a situation that initially will exist only in our minds, in our heads, in our imagination. As we conjure up a vision of a better situation ahead, and "see" it, so we become better informed for working out the route to get there. The metaphor used is that of a journey, with you the reader represented as the traveller. Metaphors are very powerful tools in "Whatever Next....?" thinking, as indeed they are in everyday thought and discussion. Author CS Lewis wrote that "all language is metaphorical through and through". We conjure up pictures with our words all the time, unless we are talking solely about what he calls "objects of sense". If you doubt that metaphors are used so frequently, remember the immortal words of Yorkshire and England cricketer Fred Trueman who was famously quoted as saying, "I don't use metaphors, I prefer plain speaking – I don't like beating about the bush!"

A metaphor, an analogy, or an actual pictorial representation on a piece of paper or a flip chart, all give us the opportunity to explore an idea without intellectually having to (or indeed wanting to!) master the detail of exactly how the situation represented came into being. This is a "safe" exercise yielding many useful and unexpected outcomes as we wander around inside our picture, gaining new perceptions of what might be going on.

A much valued part of "Whatever Next....?" workshops is the drawing of such pictures, particularly depictions of where you are now and where you want to be in the future. Artistic talent is not required! All that's needed is for *you* to understand the picture and to explain it to another. Such a picture will actually tell you a great deal about what the future will be *like*, how it will be the same and how it will be different from your "now" picture. Try this exercise for yourself. Once drawn, show the two pictures to someone else and describe what they mean and why various features are important to you. Then encourage questions from them on why aspects of the picture are as they are, and explore the metaphor that you have just created for yourself. Many hidden truths, motivations, longings and insights will emerge from this exercise if you follow it through.

Metaphors (of which journeys are a good example) give us the chance to find out what we want in a different way. The epigram "I want never gets" may well have featured in your childhood, especially if you are of my vintage! But that saying was always intended as a lesson in good *manners*, pointing us to the word "please", and not intended to squash our ability to express our real desires clearly. Sadly, however, it has had exactly that cultural effect, particularly for the British, rendering us less than adept at saying what we really want! A metaphorical picture, in words or felt tips, neatly bypasses that particularly unhelpful hang-up.

The other aspect of metaphor is the ability that it gives us to unfold the story, map or picture to show us what else is just around the corner, over the horizon or beyond our vision at the moment. The fact is that your story and my story are parts of a much bigger story. We need to visualise elements from the bigger story, or bigger picture, to give our picture an orientation and a sense of purpose, direction and ultimate meaning.

Developing the ability to enjoy the journey is vital. If we are only concerned with destination, product, outcome or solution, we are missing so much. We become interested only in tomorrow at the expense of today. By being constantly engaged with getting the future sewn up, we lose much of the joy of the present moment, the "being me, right now" and the engagement with today's issues. Events are transitory by nature and so are our experiences – they are not principles by which we live nor are they purely means to an end. We need "rocks" to stand on and a "true north" to guide us, and then we can *enjoy* the transition....right now! Getting there can indeed be fun!

The prevailing emphasis on ends, destination or product is partly a phenomenon of the rampant consumer culture in which so much of the world is immersed. We want "it", and preferably right now – we don't want the earning of it, the working at it, the striving for it, the yearning for it. Yet all these are part of a mountain to climb (new metaphor!) that make "it" all worthwhile and worth reaching. I guess the summit of a mountain alone, unsupported by foothills, would fall back to sea level! What satisfaction could anyone gain by standing on that?

Direction comes into navigation frequently, almost by definition. When we are journeying, the question "Which way?" will frequently be asked or implied. If we are not to wander aimlessly, we need to know where we are heading in the longer term and that may well bring us back to an issue of faith. *Do* we know where we are heading? Can we know? St. John in one of his letters gives us all sorts of different "yes" answers to that question. St. Paul writes to the Colossians that they are called "heavenwards" – that suggests an upward sense of direction which was foreshadowed many times in the ancient scriptures of the Old Testament hundreds of years earlier, notably by Solomon:

The path of life leads upward for the wise.

Whatever our age and stage in life we need some definite sense of purpose and direction and will be the poorer without it. Without such a sense, our enjoyment of the actual travelling may frequently be disturbed. The journey itself could well prove frustrating and pointless if we are not even sure that we are pointed in the right general direction.

Whether this direction is derived from a pre-set course based on compass points, a strong religious faith (or a weak one!), a trust in a person or a sense of what we want to achieve on this earth, we will continue to wonder (and wander!) without it.

The secret surely is not to settle on "it" too soon, and to feel able to explore alternatives within a safe framework. That framework or architecture is exactly what "Whatever Next....?" in its various forms aims to provide.

Questions to ponder:

What is your metaphor for where you are now and for where you would like to be?

Can you draw or describe it here?

Notes:

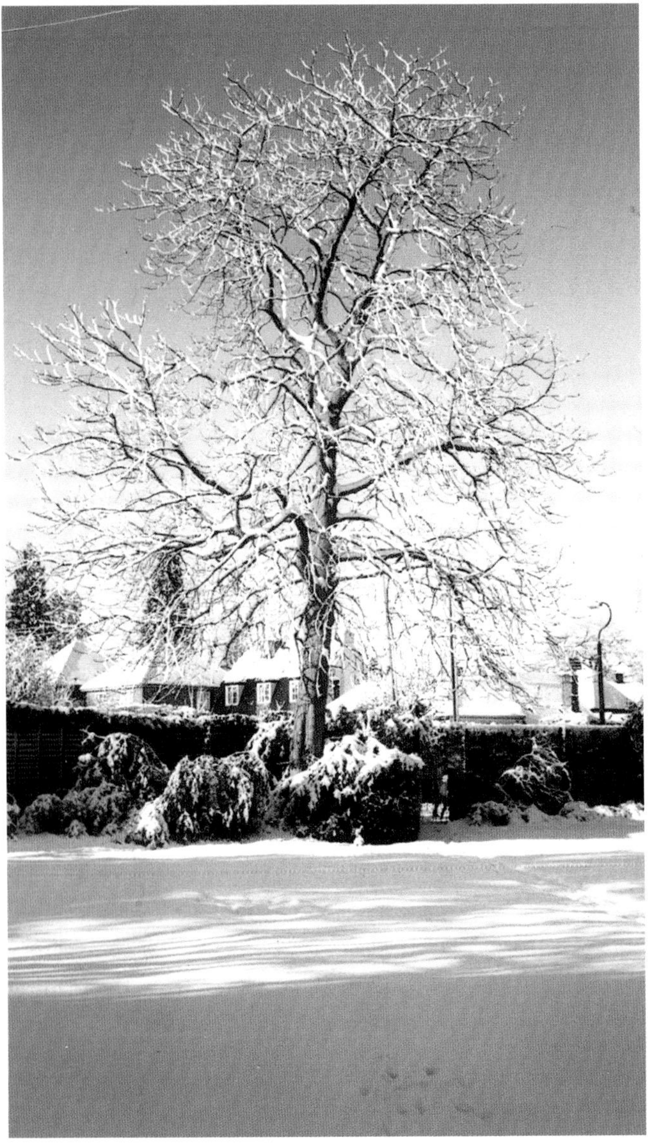

Chapter 6

Help

(Season: "Winter" Key question: "Where shall I start?")

I have already referred to 17th century poet John Donne's famous assertion that "No man is an island complete unto itself". Over the years many British people have seemed particularly keen to overthrow that notion! Examples include the idea of the self-made man, the extolling of independence as the ultimate virtue, and the siege mentality implied by the imagery of the home as an Englishman's castle (often found in my part of the world behind the ramparts of high laurel hedges – we even have some ourselves!). Not quite as eloquent as Donne, but just as famously in recent years, you may remember that former Prime Minister Margaret Thatcher declared words to the effect that "there's no such thing as society".

My experience with "Whatever Next....?" has reinforced what is implied by John Donne, that we all need one another. During the workshops we have run over the last five years we have repeatedly been struck by the extent to which we can help one another if only we give ourselves the opportunity to do so! It has been rewarding to watch individuals share their experiences and insights to great effect, once traditional reserve has been overcome.

The job market today is fragmented and becoming increasingly so, especially in comparison with a century or more ago. Here's a wonderful example of the good old days...... in 1803 England created a full-time Civil Service position calling solely for a man to stand on the white cliffs of Dover with a telescope, and to ring a bell if he saw Napoleon's fleet coming. That position was not finally abolished until 1945!

The ways in which we can earn our living today are becoming more and more diverse year by year. How can we possibly know all there is to know, or even what we *need* to know, as we venture out to seek fresh employment? The irony is that a veritable plethora of raw information becomes ever more available, especially for those connected to the Internet. The associated problem is that this river of information is rapidly turning from a flow to a flood. Before long it seems as if it could become a deluge that will swamp us all! Sorting out the wheat from the chaff has become a major task in itself. A vast quantity of unsolicited junk mail, both paper and electronic, adds to the problem.

A client facing career change said to me recently that he had little difficulty with the factual, informational and analytical sides of his busy job in the City. He had been extremely successful financially in his chosen field during his twenties and early thirties. What he felt he lacked for the future was *wisdom.* By this I think he meant the consistent judgement with which to sort out what was genuinely important for him (at a personal and organisational level) from that which was generally useful, nice to know or just plain irrelevant. In the year 2000 we are dealing with ever increasing complexity, multiple conflicts and paradoxes and frightening possibilities, some of them stemming from the misuse or abuse of technology. How are we to be wise in knowing that to which we should pay attention?

None of us has a monopoly of wisdom. That may be a well-worn cliché, but it is a useful and apt one. George Eliot, the Victorian novelist, wrote:

What do we live for if not to make life less difficult for one another?

This thought could be considered part of the very ethos of "Whatever Next....?". If we tell our story out loud, then another person can see, hear and perceive that story very differently from the way we perceive it, and then share with us their fresh perspective. Now note this carefully, **complex problems do not necessarily require complex solutions**. It may not require peculiar insight or particularly sharp minds for a crucially important remark to be forthcoming, after we have told and illustrated our story and invited comments from helpful, supportive people. We can even get crucial insights from difficult, unsupportive people, if we are prepared to accept them!

We can "see" a story in a completely different way when we speak it out, "put it on the table", get on the outside of it and just look at it again. We can then think some more about it, but in a different way. "Ponder anew....." is a very favourite expression of mine, borrowed from a well known 17th century hymn by Joachim Neander.

Of one thing I am now absolutely certain: wisdom does not consist of working out how to fit even more information and activity into our lives. That is the false dawn heralded by many so-called "time management" courses. Genuine wisdom may well lead us to do less and not more. If that is to be so, and I know it sounds attractive to many people, then wisdom will need to show us what it is "right" for us to do. Right in this context is closely allied to the concept of the life direction we steer that was examined in the previous chapter. It crucially needs to become our *own* concept of what keeps us on track, both at work and at home, and particularly in busy or stormy times.

It's a shame we cannot sit down now and watch a section of this video together, but many readers will remember the film comedy *City Slickers*, in which New York executive types head out West to cowboy country to "find themselves" on a cattle drive, far removed from their normal hectic lifestyles. Curly, the shrewd, tough, hard-bitten trail boss observes cannily:

"Yep, y'all come up here about the same time. Same age, same problems. Spend about 50 weeks of the year getting knots in yer rope and then y' think two weeks up here will untie 'em all for you. None of you get it, do you? Do y' know what the secret of life is?"

"No........what?" (coming from Billy Crystal's character, a middle-aged advertising executive)

"This" says Curly, holding up a single finger,

"Your finger?"

*"No", says Curly, "One thing! Just **one thing** you stick to that and everything else don't mean shit"*

"That's great!" says Billy Crystal scornfully, "But what's the one thing?"

*"**That's** what you've come to figure out"*

Let's take a giant leap from Arizona to the Middle East and from the end of the 20th century (when City Slickers was such a big hit) to 30 AD or thereabouts. How on earth did Jesus Christ, an exceptionally busy and able person, do what he did? How did he know what was the one thing to tackle at each time of each day? He knew himself that he couldn't and shouldn't do everything that people called on him to do. He also knew that he couldn't do any of it at all on his own. He needed general guidelines from the ancient wisdom of the scriptures and also sought his Father's daily guidance on specific choices. That guidance concerned both the issues of the day itself and also the long-term future. Jesus said of the Holy Spirit, the abiding presence of God:

He will tell you what is to come

I don't know what your views are about Jesus, but just consider this for a moment. If Jesus didn't either desire or claim to be totally self-sufficient, even though it appears that he could have been given his supernatural abilities, then why do we? Individuals, churches and indeed society in general all suffer from periods of ineffectiveness. This is partly brought about by the failure to pool all types of resources and in so doing to invest in one another in a positive, creative and expectant manner.

Questions to ponder:

Do I have problems talking to other people about the things I want to change?

Am I willing to be helped along the way or does that bother me?

What are the real obstacles to sharing the issues?

What sort of wisdom do I particularly need – who might help?

Notes:

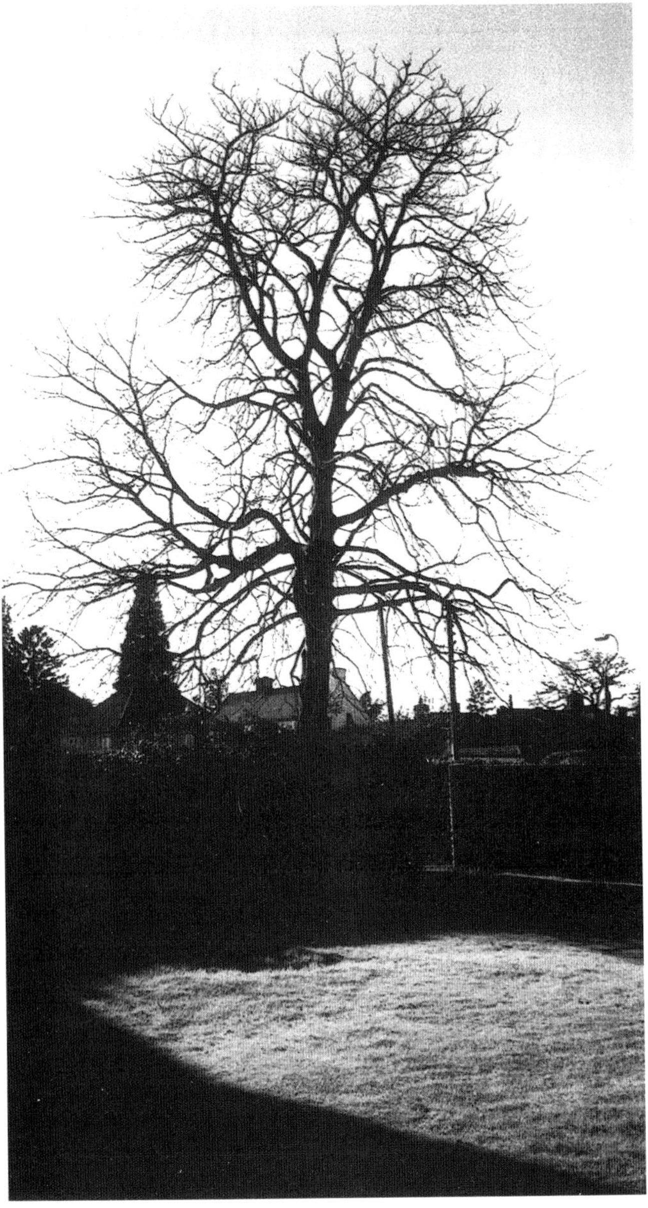

Chapter 7

Perception

(Season: "Spring" Key question: "How do I get there?")

William James, brother of novelist Henry James, once said that "the greatest discovery of the twentieth century is that we can alter our lives by altering our attitude". I'm not sure whether we are really the first generation to know this, nor am I certain whether or not our more deep-rooted problems can be altered permanently by adopting a different attitude. However, I do believe that he was onto something of great value!

As Mike O'Sullivan and I have spent time with a whole variety of people who are ready to award themselves adequate space and time to ponder constructively on their circumstances, again and again we have seen them turn keys and unlock a situation. This has most often been achieved by taking a different view of that same set of circumstances.........from which they gain a changed perspective.......... and then an improved attitude.

This is not an intellectual, analytical, problem-solving exercise, puzzling out what is wrong and immediately putting it right. It is more a willingness quite simply to go to another place, to join a colleague perhaps, and just to look again ....to ponder anew. **In order to do that it requires you to get your own issue out "on the table" where you and others can see it.** That, in itself, is a considerable step. You are now looking at a more stationary picture, as if viewed from the outside in, rather than trying to examine the situation while it actually buzzes around in your head like an angry bluebottle, constantly on the move!

If that is the very first step on this journey, then what of the more usual meeting protocols whereby we set up our agenda for addressing all the issues, and then decide how to cover that agenda? We do not need that particular protocol in the "Whatever Next....?" approach. There are places for such pre-meditated agendas in business-oriented situations with limited time and the need for snappy decisions. Intriguingly, however, my actual experience over the years (gained in government service, business, social and church settings) is that the presence of a pre-fixed agenda does little either to shorten a meeting or to improve the quality of decisions made. It often serves to increase the *quantity* of decisions that need to be made, and nearly always the amount of discussion that surrounds each one!

Time and again we have experienced the value of *not* having an agenda at the beginning of a "Whatever Next....?" day, of being encouraged to speak out the previously unspoken, to voice the unmentionable, to explore the unreachable and to describe the unfathomable. This has most often been done through stories, pictures, metaphors and other imagery.

Yes, of course, this a very different way of approaching issues, but then if you always do what you always did, you'll always get what you always got! Doing things the same way again and again will eventually limit the ways in which we are *able* to think about them.

To those who may doubt their own ability to embrace such a radical change, I refer them to Alfred, Lord Tennyson, in the poem Ulysses,

Come my friends, 'tis not too late to seek a newer world
(and note especially the "not too late" bit!)

Let's return now to William James, with whom we started the chapter. A different attitude is required in order to embrace, or at least explore, a new idea. No fixed doctrine or message is being imposed – no change is being wrenched from you, or forced into you. Look back at Maurice Maeterlinck quoted in the Foreword. He says that if a situation is accurately perceived, change will start to happen as night follows day. We are consequently freed up to ask "Whatever Next....?"

General Douglas MacArthur, famous American commander in the Second World War and thereafter, wrote this:

Whatever your years, there is in every heart the love of wonder, the undaunted challenge of events, the unfailing child-like appetite for what comes next. You are as young as your hope and as old as your despair.

A new view gives us a completely new opportunity, a chance to think differently about a seemingly familiar situation. A new perception can change us forever. This insight of itself is nothing new. St. Paul wrote nearly two thousand years ago that we can be transformed by the renewing of our minds. In other words if we can think differently, we can become different.

A creative way to think about the future, therefore, may be to de-emphasise the well-worn agendas and to be more conscious of the value of good process. We need to be stronger on *how* we are going to live and to be gentler with ourselves on exactly where we feel we have to get to. Increasing our self-awareness is necessary for such changes of emphasis. We will need much more honest and under-standable measurements of *what* we are, *who* we are and *where* we are in our lives, and much less emphasis on our relative importance and status measured purely in political, business or social terms.

Back to Tennyson, and the epic poem Ulysses:

That which we are, we are,
One equal temper of heroic hearts, made weak by time and
fate but strong in will,
To strive, to seek, to find and not to yield.

Is this stanza about process or product, is it about jour-ney or destination, is it about the being or the doing? I believe it is primarily about the former in each case, even though there are elements of achievement implied. Societal and commercial emphasis in the 21st century leans very much more on our track record of tangible, measurable (and usually financial!) results than on how we got there – the "bottom line" rules, OK?

Well no, actually.......I want to say vehemently that it's *not* always OK for the bottom line to rule! To give a different flavour to the discussion, we are told by St. James in his own New Testament letter that "Faith without works is dead" (from which it might seem that "works" might be the bottom line!) but we also told by Paul that "without faith it is impossible to please God" (in other words that the *process* is vital!). There's a healthy balance to be struck in all this between what we achieve and how we achieve it.

Let's close this chapter by proposing that life's multiple journeys are, or can be perceived to be, exciting and fulfill-ing experiences. In proposing this, however, let's also note that if we have, perhaps subconsciously, always put major life transitions and changes into a brain-file marked "unpleasant, and to be avoided wherever possible" – then that is how they will tend to turn out. We will be pre-programmed for a painful trip!

Questions to ponder:

What is the key issue that I want to ponder anew?

What is my current view of this issue (description or picture)?

How might I look at it differently?

Notes:

Chapter 8

Principles

(Season: "Spring" Key question: "How do I get there?")

It would be reasonable to suppose that the countries of Western Europe and North America do not play host to the highest levels of poverty, disease, exploitation, hunger or natural disasters. They are, however, widely reputed to host the highest levels of individual stress in the world, and particularly stress-related illnesses. This seeming anomaly is worth reflecting upon, and perhaps discussing with someone right now, especially if you are reading this alongside someone else. Simply reflect, "Why might this be so?"

I can suggest one major contributory reason for the high stress levels. We give ourselves very little time to get our hurried and hurrying lives into any sort of perspective. Jesus Christ said on a number of occasions to his close followers "Come with me to a quiet place.........". There are some forty instances of this type of "withdrawal" related in the gospels. This encouragement to slow down for a while came from a man who had been tasked, at the age of 30, with turning the entire world upside down forever in just 3 years, helped by 12 untrained and relatively uneducated assistants! Surely we can learn something from that.

Indeed it informs the **first principle of "Whatever Next....?"**: *that we need to take more time to consider ourselves.* In practice that may well involve more regular times to reflect on our situation, perhaps to meditate or pray if we find that helpful, and then from that reflection to consider both what we intend to do and how we might go about it.

The **second principle**, mentioned briefly in Chapter 7, is that having set aside the time we *begin the process by getting the first thoughts concerning our issues out in front of us (spoken or in writing), where we can see them*. If others can see or hear them too, then so much the better.

The **third principle** is that *the more we now "unfold the map" (i.e. explore our story), and reveal other aspects, the more the uniqueness of our own situation becomes apparent*. In addition to this, more opportunities are afforded to spot patterns or metaphors that we have never seen previously while we have been staring at it from the inside.

The first three principles can now be summed up in a single paragraph:

Take some good quality time with at least one other person (each of you having a copy of this book) and simply tell them the story of whatever it is that you want to address. Explore together the edges of the story or picture. Unfold those boundaries, in order to see more of the possible origins and destinations of the narrative that you have now told and perhaps illustrated.

The fourth principle is the hardest to digest at first, so chew it over really well before trying to swallow it!

You are exactly where you have chosen to be at this moment in time.

This is a deep and difficult premise to accept, and especially so if we perceive our current situation to be pretty dire. But a word of caution – think very carefully before rejecting it because within it are the seeds of our own free will.

I am not going to shy away from a tough example - I guess that you will rightly come up with one if I don't! Consider, as if it were today, the refugees from Kosovo pouring into the Albanian and Macedonian refugee camps in 1999, a very recent memory when I first wrote these words. Am I saying that they really *chose* to be there? Well, think about it - at various points in the previous days, weeks, months or years those refugees had to make choices. They chose *not* to engage in hand to hand combat, *not* to collaborate with the "enemy", and *not* to hide in cellars or mountains. They chose, albeit in appalling circumstances, to remain free and to walk out of their own country into another. The circumstances were appalling but those people were still free and alive. We now know that later on many of them chose to walk on elsewhere, or to walk back to rebuild their shattered homes. There *were* choices involved throughout but not necessarily, of course, were they agreeable, easy or obvious choices.

Let's return from that tough and harrowing scenario to the here and now. If you are, so far, unconvinced by this fourth principle, just park your response for now and reflect on it again later. It's helpful to do that sometimes, just to park our thoughts where they are for the time being and unfold more of the map to see where we might go next.

Whatever your circumstances, however discouraging or distressing, you always retain and can always exercise one choice – how to react both to the circumstances and to those who perpetrate them. That choice may not always include physical freedoms of manoeuvre, but it will always apply to the way you think about what is happening to you.

How did you get to where you are today? I think you got to where you are by a series of choices, some proactive and positive, others reactive and possibly negative (in the sense that you chose *not* to do something or *not* to go somewhere else). Some choices will have been straightforward, almost instinctive; others will have been agonised over, seemingly forever. Some will have been logical, others crazy. **But they will have been your choices.**

Before you protest that your situation today is "not your fault", remove from the argument altogether the concepts of blame and fault and then think again:

Are you where you are today because of a series of events in which you were a participant?

Is it reasonable to suggest that you have had at least some element of choice (very possibly not all that you wanted) in that series of events?

Are there a number of different ways in which you can now react to your current situation?

If the answer to these questions is yes, then the fourth principle does stand firm for further exploration. If the answer is no, it appears that you are purely a spectator at the ringside of life's circus. It may well feel exactly like that as you read this............ but thankfully it's not true! Be reassured that you belong in the ring with all the rest of us, and you are still very much part of the action.

If we can now accept that this fourth principle stands i.e. that we are where we have chosen to be, then we are indeed truly free. We are free to explore a different perspective on our own "Whatever Next....?" questions, namely that if we

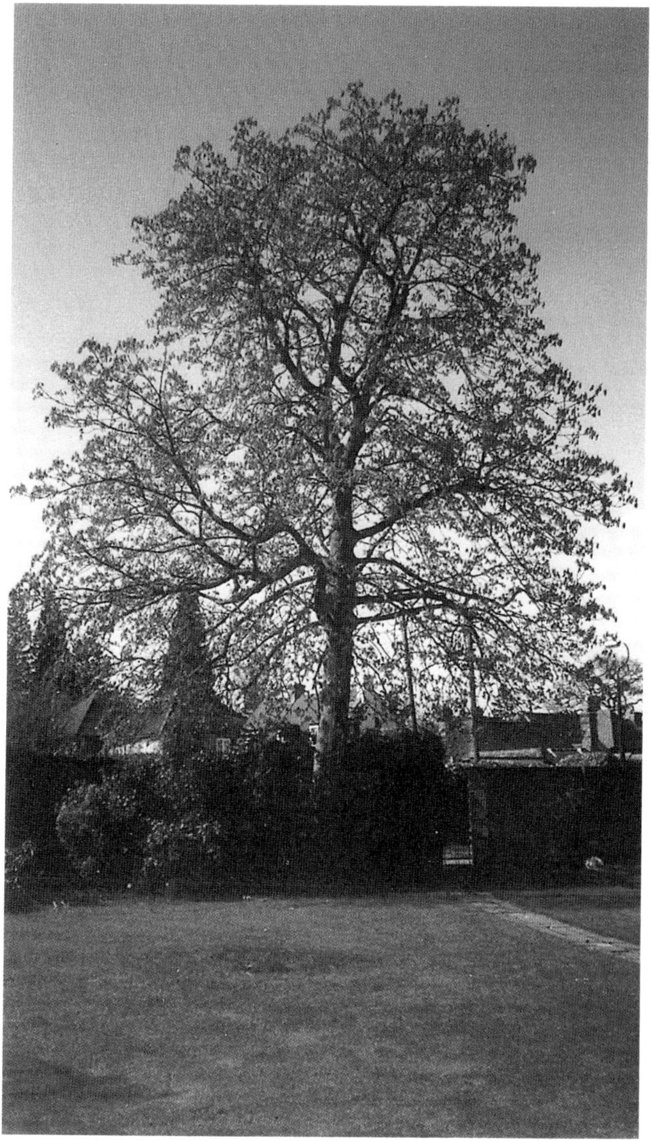

chose our way *in* to this situation then it follows that we can choose our way *out.* If we did not, and cannot (for we were brought here by fate, bad luck, stars etc!) then what hope have we got anyway?

And so to the last two principles:

The **fifth principle** is that *creativity is required to do something entirely new, and that such creativity must involve stepping out into the unknown.* How else can we travel new ground? Stepping out in the knowledge that we have free will in our attitude (even if not always in action) means that we are all able to move on from where we are now. We don't have to know exactly where we are going to. We can just continue the journey in the right general direction and continue to seek guidance until the precise destination becomes clearer. Always remember that the journey is, *in itself,* creative.

Continuing the journey will by definition result in us getting different views, both forwards and backwards. If we stay exactly where we are, we plainly cannot get those new perspectives and indeed may not be able to see what we need to see. As we move and see things from a new angle, solutions have a way of revealing themselves – and this indeed is the **sixth and last principle** of "Whatever Next....?" *Solutions do indeed have a way of revealing themselves.* Strange but true!

All this is representative of a growing and developing process, and in writing it down I am immediately conscious of changing the metaphor, away from that of a journey! Out of the difficult and dark soil where we felt stuck, we can now begin to recognise that new shoots are sprouting. They are growing from the seeds that were planted just by looking afresh at our own story.

I want to add that this process is in no way a denigration of the value of the past! We have all been where we have been, and we are what we are largely because of that past. Recrimination, blame and fault are not going to illuminate the picture or the story or the way ahead. Forgiveness, acceptance and new life are all going to help provide the light which we need to step out on the path on which we *now* choose to travel.

Please note that these six principles are not any sort of holy writ. You may well accept some more easily than others. You may want to add some principles of your own. This would be entirely in the spirit of "Whatever Next....?" We have found thus far, however, that these six basic ideas work well for people in practice, and we also believe them to have sound foundations both in psychology and the wisdom literature of many different traditions.

Questions to ponder:

Having explored your story and any issues with a friend or colleague, ask yourself:

Where am I now?

What choices that I made in the past contributed to the issues I'm now facing?

In what ways could I consider stepping out into the unknown?

Notes:

Chapter 9

Processes

(Season: "Spring" Key question: "How do I get there?")

I am not sure where they came from, but I have just read these words that I scribbled on a scrap of paper a few days ago:

I am sharing what I am learning en route

On reflection as I start to write this chapter, that is exactly what the "Whatever Next....?" approach is about. I am sharing in these pages what I am actually in the process of learning for myself – that is all I am doing and that is all I want you to do: to share your story and reflect on what you are learning as you do so.

Now for some I suspect that this idea on its own may be just a little too vague for them! Take heart, however, because in this chapter and the next I hope to supply you with both the basic thought processes and some practical guidance as to how to work in this "Whatever Next....?" mode with others.

Process 1 Telling our story

The basic idea of telling our story was introduced earlier, specifically in Chapter 7 in talking about the ways in which we can change our perceptions. The key word here in Process 1 is the *telling*. Thinking about our story is not what's required! The process is simply to decide which area(s) of our life we want to work on, and then to decide on the initial scope and timescale of exactly what we want to relate to others at the outset. Having thought about it that much, just tell it out and watch what happens!

Process 2 Listening to another story

This is not a one-way, single-focus exercise – we need some of the richer perspectives provided by other stories and by the people who are sharing them. We need the discipline of giving others "a good listening to" as well as hearing our own voice! The process at this early stage is merely to listen and then briefly to clarify points about which you may be unclear. No problem solving please!

These two processes need to come first in the day, but after that any or all of the following processes may be appropriate, in any order.

Process 3 Unfolding the story or picture and making it bigger

Wherever the story stops there will be an edge or a boundary to manage. The next helpful process is to unfold some of the edges and see what else can be discovered. This may happen naturally as a result of the first round of clarifying comments or questions. Otherwise, some questions along the lines of "What else?", "What then?" "What happened next?" "What happened before that?" will elicit this unfolding of the memory and the perception. Remember that there is no necessity to answer a question just because it has been asked. There should be no requirement for pressure to be applied or felt by anyone. Questions asked but not answered are just as powerful.

Process 4 Landmarks and orientation

Sometimes it's helpful to perceive the story in a wider context and as part of a bigger story. For instance, there are different ages and stages in all our lives that call for different perspectives. Perhaps we are trying to decide what's next in our work. The decision and the exploration may well need to be referenced to other known points and people in our lives – the thought to be developed is one of our relationship with other fixed points. In physical geography it is possible to read a map well on paper and to know what all the symbols mean, and yet be unable to relate this picture accurately to what can be seen on the ground, in the real world.

Process 5 Clarifying and refining

This relates to the way in which we need better to understand our story or someone else's, especially when we have just heard it for the first time. The best way is for other people to ask us questions to clarify it for them. This results in explanations, refinements and additions that then proceed to clarify it for us! We probably don't need people to tell us what to do next; we are more likely just to need people to tell us what they see in our story or our picture. They do not need to be "right" in order to be helpful.

It is worth noting that most people with some degree of experience in life need *reminding* of key factors more than to be taught them as if they were new boys or girls at school!

Process 6 **Focusing on the process and not fretting about the outcome**

This is *so* important. The time for the outcome may not be today. Concentrate on today's process, which may, in itself, be a completely new experience for you. Enjoying each other's company and the stories themselves is all part of what may be most valuable to you. The answer to your key issue is not the thing to aim for throughout the day. Help each other all you can to clarify their perception, and then let the changes needed follow, as and when.

Notes:

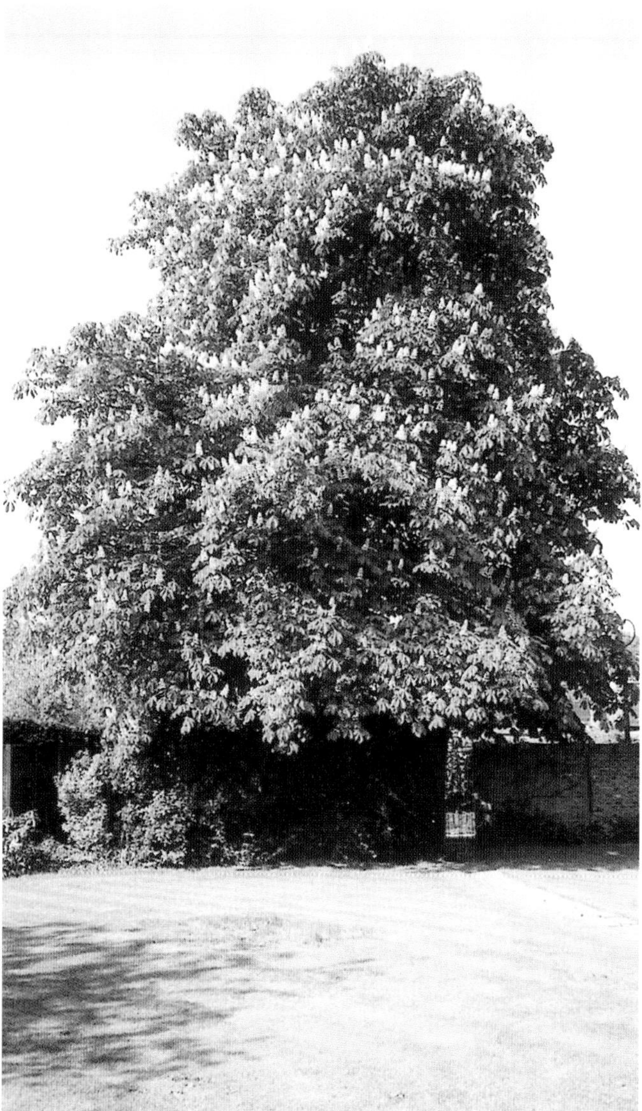

Chapter 10

Practice

(Season : "Summer" Keynote question: "What shall I do now?")

Someone wisely observed that often the past itself is not our problem; rather it's the pattern that our past has set up in our present: it is the way that the past has preconditioned our thinking today.

Now we come on to some practical matters as to how we can set up the practice of "Whatever Next....?" principles and processes (Chapters 8 and 9). If you have chosen to leap into the book right here, then you are probably more interested in doing it, not just knowing about it or understanding the thinking behind it. So you are going to set aside some time for simply getting on with the process. If you find that this chapter doesn't make as much sense to you as you would like, dip into some of the other chapters and see whether that helps you to get started. You will find Chapter 9 particularly useful, as it outlines some of the processes you can use in your day of exploration.

My initial suggestion for a really worthwhile "Whatever Next....?" session is to set aside not less than half a day and preferably a whole working day of 7 or 8 hours.

Immediate reaction from busy people is often that they would prefer a half-hour version – I'm afraid it's just not available! "Whatever Next....?" is unashamedly reflective and reflection takes time. A practical tip towards making it happen: if you put the session into your diary a few weeks hence, then you will soon get attuned to the idea of protecting it and you will also have better opportunities to identify the issues you want to bring out on the day itself. You will need to interest at least one other person in doing the same and give them a copy of the book, if they haven't got one already. Later on you may be able to use a few of the "Whatever Next....?" principles working entirely on your own but while you are getting familiar with the processes identified in earlier chapters, you very much need the collective approach. All those taking part need to commit to seeing the time through, no late starts or early finishes.

Treat it like an exceptionally important meeting, because it is just that!

Find a good place to meet. It should be quiet, relatively uninterrupted, and preferably an attractive venue where it is enjoyable just to be there. Why not book somewhere special and different? The process will seldom be as effective when conducted in your own front room or office, with all the familiar cues around you which signal that other work is just waiting to be done! Leave mobile phones behind.

An encouraging symptom at this very early stage is a feeling of excitement and anticipation, even well ahead of the chosen day. That usually increases at the beginning of the day itself and remarks like "I've never spent any concentrated time thinking about my own life" are commonplace. You are going to make use of the energy you have created *just by setting aside the time* – the day is *already* a success, you're there!

Find comfortable seating and a pad of blank paper,

preferably large size – there's nothing quite like the power which is generated by starting such a day with a completely blank flip-chart pad and absolutely no agenda – the medium is the message!

Have a discussion at the outset on confidentiality between the participants. This can take one of two forms; either complete or non-existent, anything in-between is ambiguous. Either take the view that nothing divulged during the day will be spoken about to anyone else outside the room without specific permission *or* that people will only talk about things that they do not mind being shared or discussed outside, if it is thought helpful and appropriate. Decide on one or the other and remind yourselves at the end of the day about that agreement.

Get started with your stories. Don't waste time trying to allocate time to other activities (except lunch perhaps!) or spend valuable time setting un-needed agendas, just go for it! Remember that this is a different approach! Stories can just be recounted verbally, in narrative form and I suggest that they are recounted in direct response to the simple question "Why have you come here today?". These are not to be whole life stories, which would be inappropriately lengthy. Suggest 10-15 minutes as a guide and then allow another 10 minutes for questions of fact or clarification only, from others present. ***Don't start probing and trying to solve the "problem".*** When the story and clarification has finished move on to the next person.

An alternative approach is to allow everyone time at the outset to draw a metaphorical picture or diagram of the story or issue they want to discuss, perhaps using coloured felt tips and a piece of flip-chart paper. This will create a different version of the story coming more from the right-hand part of the brain, the creative, spatial bit. Either method is fine, both work well. People then take their 10 minutes to describe the picture, what it means and what is significant about various features they have drawn. The others can then ask brief questions, as before, to clarify points.

By this time everyone should be well into the process and engaged with each other to some extent; that will deepen as the day goes on.

The picturing exercise, also outlined in Chapter 5, can be used later in the day to depict where participants are trying to get to. If people enjoy working this way it's always a welcome change from talking and listening for the whole time. The great thing to remember about pictures and metaphors is that what comes out onto a piece of paper is partly unconscious and instinctive rather than logical, well analysed and ordered. It gives us a completely different language to use. The interruption that this causes in our brain will disturb our more familiar patterns of communication and will be a real help both in seeing things differently and also in helping others "see" it. Look back at what was said in Chapter 5 about changing perspectives as we travel.

Another comforting feature is that these rough-drawn pictures are a very unthreatening way of communicating either all or part of your story. They usually produce much thought and laughter as well as providing useful new insights into the situation you are describing. All that is required is a simple, not necessarily artistic, drawing. We can all then look and interpret what we see, following a description by the drawer. Pictures often only *point the way* to solutions – an answer contained within our own picture still has to be spotted even after we have drawn it. Solutions have a way of revealing themselves. We've noticed that the solution is nearly always more striking to participants if it is revealed to them in an instant, rather than worked out.

As an example of this, the question "Why didn't I get that promotion?" is probably not best answered by someone else giving you a logical, well-argued reason as an immediate response. It will be much more powerful if we suddenly "see" it for ourselves, perhaps through reflection on our own picture, perhaps by the way we told our own story. We might discover not only that effectively we *chose* not to go for that promotion, but also the real reason why we chose not to.

Now an important word on outcomes. Having set this precious time aside, we all want the day to be a "success". As a consequence of this, it's sometimes very tempting to push for closure on the issues which were raised by participants in their stories at the beginning of the day. Such is the very results-oriented nature of our world!

Participation in many iterations of this "Whatever Next....?" approach leads me to believe that only part of the eventual result will be seen on the day, and indeed sometimes what is apparently only a small part. That no longer worries us at all, because we have seen time and again that an invaluable process has started which carries on ...and on! We sometimes hear weeks or months after the day itself, how various issues were resolved and exactly how this day's processes influenced events. The solutions will follow in due course. There *is* a right time for every purpose.

The telling, illustrating, questioning and refining of

personal stories are the basic building blocks of the day, indeed of the whole approach.

Let me finish the "practice" chapter by mentioning four other useful activities that can be used in support of the basic story-telling technique.

These can be used as follow-up activities later in the same day or on another day:

– take a wander in the grounds or garden and just reflect quietly on your story – pondering anew.

– in your thoughts take a wander into the future, look back down the years to the present, retrace your steps and notice how you got there from where you are today.

– start composing a written personal mission statement which states quite succinctly what your life is going to be all about in future.

– draw a picture of how you would like things to be in a year's time and then consider it.

Finish up by telling each other where you are now in your thinking at this closing point of the "Whatever Next....?" day itself. You will certainly be at a different place from where you started. Acknowledge and appreciate, out loud preferably, how each of the others have helped you move on during the day.

Please continue to ponder!

You might like to write a summary of what you enjoyed about the day and what you think you learnt from it. Don't consider this process complete, the process works best if you keep the questions open rather than thinking you have found all the answers.

Make a list of some of the things you might *like* to do next (omitting the shoulds and oughts!)

Notes:

Chapter 11

All yours

(Season: "Summer" Key question: "Where are you right now?")

The pages that follow, white and clean, may well be the most important chapter in the book for you by the time you have finished. Use the space, following some of the principles and processes outlined in this book, to map out in words and pictures some of your own thoughts and feelings as you travel this transitional territory of "Whatever Next....?".

Bob Dylan, in the lyrics of the song *Chimes of Freedom*, wrote that the bells were tolling. In particular, he felt that they were:

Tolling for the tongues with no place to put their thoughts,
Tied down in taken-for-granted situations

So....here's a chapter to write yourself. Nothing in this space need be "taken-for-granted", so take your time, be patient with yourself...........untie your tongue, and your pen, and see what happens:

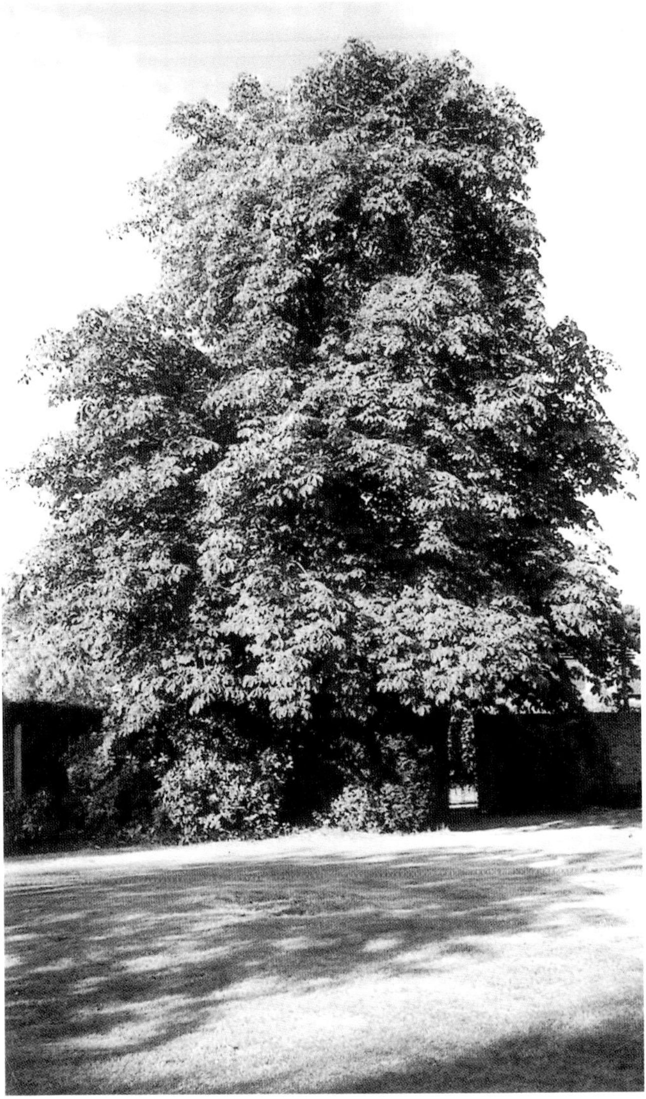

Chapter 12

What now and what else?

(Season: "Summer" Key question: " What else do I need?")

In this final chapter (not final of course if you started midway!) we will be looking at some of the reasons why "Whatever Next....?" works as it does.

As I mentioned in the introduction, my own journey has led me along a Christian path. Why have I found those teachings so helpful? Well, it has struck me for many years that Jesus was a man with a mission, but that intriguingly he didn't start that mission immediately he reached adulthood. He seemed to know in outline by the age of 12 what his mission was, yet he waited another eighteen years to get started. When he started his ministry at about the age of thirty he knew exactly what to do, and also when to do it.

He had none of the communication systems, planning aids and office-based paraphernalia that we now seem to consider essential to any major undertaking. He was given a mission which would involve changing the world irreversibly, making his presence felt throughout the earth, and leaving a legacy which is still alive throughout the world 2000 years later. He taught authoritatively by word of mouth using direct speech, metaphor and parable. He also carried out many memorable acts of goodwill and healing. He moved confidently and with great purpose from one situation to another. Jesus seemed to know exactly what to do next.

In 1977, singer-songwriter Paul Simon wrote soulfully in his marvellous song *Slip slidin' away*:

God only knows, God makes his plan, the information's unavailable to the mortal man

And yet Amos, the Old Testament prophet, contradicts that by writing that God *does* reveal his thoughts to men.

"Whatever Next....?", through its reflective patterns and processes, will help to reveal a great deal to anyone who takes the time to follow through. Remember that events are, by nature, transitory. Circumstances at this moment in time may be really good for you, or perhaps they are not so good. Even Jesus himself experienced those same swings between all seeming to be well and everything appearing to go wrong. What he knew without doubt was that God was in control.

Many are the plans in a man's heart but it is the Lord's purpose that prevails

wrote Solomon in the Proverbs.

With respect to the journey metaphor explained in detail in Chapter 5, it is worth noting that Jesus undertook his journey with what must have been a forbidding knowledge of events to come. He said once to his followers "I know where I came from *and* I know where I'm going". *How* did he know? Well, he listened to what his Father had to say to him each day.

I believe that listening will pay off for you, regardless of whether you consider yourself a believer or not. The acts of listening carefully, and perceiving accurately what we hear, underpin the "Whatever Next....?" approach and help it to work. It is that act of listening more carefully..........listening to silence, listening to ourselves and listening to other supportive people........that allows us to hear new wisdom and, I believe, allows God to have a say in the proceedings! This is especially true in the discipline of choosing to be quieter than normal. The wise King Solomon makes a staggering and wonderful promise:

Whoever listens to God will live in safety, and be at ease, without fear of harm.

Secure, at ease and without being afraid. It sounds like a very good way to be, at least most of the time! You may or may not think of yourself as a religious or spiritual person, but if these various thoughts ring a few bells with you then it's because they are resonating with the reality of your spiritual nature.

What we will all be able to hear in the gaps and spaces provided by "Whatever Next....?" is our inner self which, sensing a rare chance to make itself heard above the noise and busyness of everyday life, speaks out clearly. We may choose not to listen; we may deny that we ever heard any such thing. But......we have the answers to our own questions deep inside us and those quiet answers may need to be listened to if we are to move on purposefully.

What you have read here is neither complicated nor new, but it could well be new to you. Oliver Wendell Holmes wrote that a mind once stretched to a new idea never returns to its original dimensions. We are facing times of perhaps unprecedented change. Bob Dylan, already quoted once, wrote in one of his most insightful and poetic songs:

May you have a strong foundation when the winds of changes shift

If you are not a Dylan fan (and perhaps you've never even heard of him!) then what about famous Irish poet, WB Yeats:

Things fall apart; the centre cannot hold. Mere anarchy is loosed upon the world

Contrast this uncompromisingly gloomy view with the calm and reassuring words of St. Paul who wrote about Jesus that:

In Him all things hold together

I have done my best to be straightforward and to write what can both be read and understood. I want "Whatever Next....?" to have provided you with some keys and I trust that the doors which you choose to unlock with them will be good doors for you. I believe that you will become better equipped to face uncertainty without fretting and without always feeling that you *have* to know the exact outcome all the time.

I sometimes refer to this whole process as helping people to make friends with the question mark.

Having made frequent and specific reference to the exact title of this book, can I explain why the details matter in the title?

"Whatever Next....?"

- **Inverted commas** – because it's a real question asked by real people, including you and me!

- **Whatever** – keeping you open to new ideas, even when you are uncertain and possibly seeking a measure of security in the status quo

- **Next** – because it's primarily concerned with decision-making in the here and now

- **Four dots....** to signify a pause, a necessary time of reflection and some considerable measure of expectancy!

- **A question mark and *not* an exclamation mark** – I want you to ponder, and not to panic!

This is not a closed book – you haven't finished it yet! If you didn't start at the beginning you may want to go to Chapter One and read around. Even if you did, the process itself will need to be revisited from time to time. Reading this book has been a step on your journey, hopefully providing you with some different ways of thinking about the unknown. In uncertain and often difficult times, I hope some of these new perspectives will be a real help to you.

Question to ponder:

What is it that I *really want* to do next?

And then what..........?

Notes: